THE SCIENCE OF A PANDEMIC

ROBIN KOONTZ

Published in the United States of America by Cherry Lake Publishing
Ann Arbor, Michigan
www.cherrylakepublishing.com

Consultants: Michael A. Stoto, Professor of Health Systems Administration and Population Health, Georgetown University School of Nursing & Health Studies; Marla Conn, ReadAbility, Inc.
Editorial direction: Red Line Editorial
Book design and illustration: Design Lab

Photo Credits: Hinochika/Shutterstock Images, cover, 1; National Museum of Health and Medicine/AP Images, 5; claffra/Shutterstock Images, 9; CDC, 13 (top left), 13 (top right), 13 (bottom left), 13 (bottom right), 29; Maps.com/Corbis, 15; Bettmann/Corbis, 18; BSIP/UIG/Getty Images, 21; National Cancer Institute/Science Faction/Corbis, 25; Shehzad Noorani/Canadian Press/AP Images, 27

Library of Congress Cataloging-in-Publication Data
Koontz, Robin Michal, author.
  The science of a pandemic / by Robin Koontz.
    pages cm. -- (Disaster science)
  Audience: Age 11.
  Audience: Grades 4 to 6.
  Includes bibliographical references and index.
  ISBN 978-1-63137-625-2 (hardcover) -- ISBN 978-1-63137-670-2 (pbk.) -- ISBN 978-1-63137-715-0 (pdf ebook) -- ISBN 978-1-63137-760-0 (hosted ebook)
  1. Epidemics--Juvenile literature. 2. Communicable diseases--Epidemiology--Juvenile literature. 3. Communicable diseases--Prevention--Juvenile literature. I. Title.

  RA653.5.K66 2015
  614.4--dc23   2014004031

Cherry Lake Publishing would like to acknowledge the work of
The Partnership for 21st Century Skills. Please visit www.p21.org
for more information.

Printed in the United States of America
Corporate Graphics Inc.
July 2014

ABOUT THE AUTHOR

Robin Koontz is an award-winning author and illustrator of a wide variety of books and articles for children and young adults. In 2011, she was an Animal Behavior Society Outstanding Children's Book Award Finalist. Koontz lives with her husband in the Coast Range of western Oregon.

TABLE OF CONTENTS

DANGERS AMONG US

A terrible disaster struck the world in 1918 and 1919. In the course of about 18 months, approximately 500 million people around the world became sick. More than 50 million people died from the worst outbreak of **influenza**, or flu, in known history. The deadly flu spread so quickly that laws were passed in an effort to slow it. It was made illegal in some public places to cough, spit, or sneeze. People wore masks when they went outside.

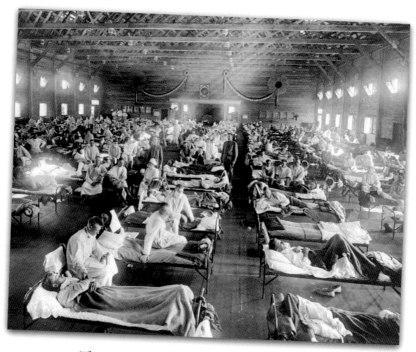

The 1918 flu pandemic left millions dead.

Masks are still an effective way to prevent the spread of a disease **microbe**. A single sneeze can send a tiny microbe all the way across a room. Some microbes can live outside a body for 48 hours or more. During that time, they can infect anyone with whom they come in contact. Unless a mask blocks them, microbes can easily invade people's bodies through the nose or mouth.

Most people have a healthy **immune system**. It works to protect us against flu viruses and other germs. We encounter potentially disease-causing microbes every day, but our immune systems are able to fight them off before they make us sick. However, if the immune system encounters a new and unusual microbe, it may be unable to effectively fight it.

Virologists, the scientists who study viruses, and epidemiologists, the scientists who study **contagious** diseases, work to keep pace with newly emerging viruses. There are many flu viruses, and they are changing all the time. This is one reason people are urged to get a flu shot every year. Vaccines, which are shots that help prevent diseases, must be constantly updated to fight off the latest flu viruses.

The Centers for Disease Control and Prevention (CDC) is the government agency responsible for public health in the United States. It defines an epidemic as the larger-than-expected presence of a disease in a particular area, likely with a common cause. If that disease spreads to a wider area, covering multiple countries or continents, it is considered a pandemic.

MODERN INFLUENZA

Robert G. Webster is a world authority on influenza. He and his research team have been studying avian, or bird, flu strains in Southeast Asia. They track new strains of flu in different birds to watch for possible pandemics. They capture the birds and test their blood. Then they compare the different kinds of viruses they find.

The deadly flu virus H5N1 surfaced in 2004 among chickens and ducks from eight countries. In two of those countries, Thailand and Vietnam, the virus also infected people. That meant the H5N1 virus had adapted to survive inside human bodies, rather than just in birds. The scientists discovered the virus was also killing wild ducks and shorebirds. Today, research teams are working with Canadian wildlife officials to test migrating birds. Migrating birds could carry a deadly virus to new areas. Because it was discovered that some strains of these viruses can survive in people, scientists believe bird migration could lead to a pandemic.

TOO CLOSE FOR COMFORT

Contagious diseases spread from one human to another because people come into close contact with each other. When this happens, viruses move from one host to another. The viruses that cause diseases such as influenza, measles, and tuberculosis are spread through the air. Touching someone who is ill, or something that they touched, can also spread a disease. Disease microbes can sometimes live for many hours outside a host. So if an infected person touches a doorknob, someone who touches it hours later may become infected.

Another way people become infected by viruses is by living close to insect or animal **vectors**. A vector is a living thing that transmits disease to another living thing. Mosquitoes are vectors for some of the most contagious diseases in the world. They have contributed to pandemics of bubonic plague and malaria. In human communities, people usually collect and store water,

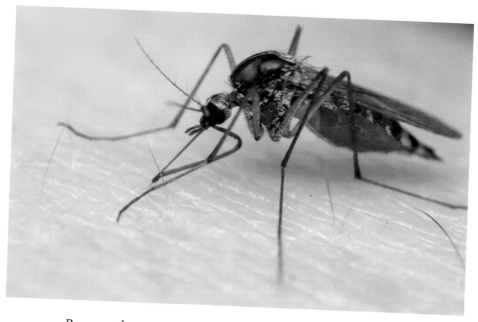

Because they spread dangerous diseases, some people have called mosquitoes the deadliest animals on Earth.

creating an environment perfect for mosquito growth. Adult mosquitoes bite animals and people in order to access their blood, which the insects use as food. In the process, mosquitoes transfer microbes to the creatures they bite. This is how they spread diseases.

Stored food can also be exposed to disease. Scavenger animals such as rats and mice, as well as their fleas, can host all kinds of nasty diseases. Hantavirus is one deadly disease spread by contact with infected rats and mice. Cows, sheep, pigs, chickens, and other domestic animals can also carry **infectious** diseases.

When an infection jumps from an animal to a human, it is called a zoonotic disease. More than half of the 1,700 known viruses, bacteria, and other microbes that infect people are zoonotic diseases.

Poor sanitation can also promote the spread of disease. Water **contaminated** with waste can carry diseases such as cholera, dysentery, and typhoid fever. If human waste is stored in unsanitary conditions, such as

Natural Reservoirs

The host or carrier of a contagious disease is called a natural reservoir. For example, mosquitoes are a natural reservoir for the disease malaria. Scientists try to determine the natural reservoirs of the viruses they discover. This helps them learn more about the life cycle of the disease and how it spreads. They can then work on ways to control the disease.

in open sewers, disease can spread. The flies that tend to live near waste can also be vectors of infectious diseases.

Human travel is one of the fastest and easiest ways for a disease to spread. People might be immune to disease microbes they have lived around all their lives. But when people travel to a new place, they are exposed to new microbes. They also bring unfamiliar microbes to the place they are visiting. An epidemic can start when a new disease is introduced to a population of people. Even a single person can potentially trigger a pandemic.

Natural disasters can also give diseases a chance to spread. When floods, earthquakes, hurricanes, and other natural disasters happen, the spread of disease can sometimes take more lives than the original disaster itself. Broken sewer lines can contaminate the clean water systems upon which people depend. New diseases can be carried in from other areas. Natural disasters often lead to shortages of food, clean water, and medical care. This can leave people more vulnerable to disease. Diseases spread in war-torn countries for similar reasons. Finally, pandemics can occur because of a lack of good medical care and transportation for ill people.

Before a vaccine can be invented, one type of virus can potentially infect millions of people. Epidemiologists and other scientists work around the clock to track, contain, and prevent the spread of disease.

THE SPREAD OF INFLUENZA

These maps show the spread of influenza in the United States between October 2013 and January 2014. It was not a pandemic, but the maps show how fast diseases can spread. Do you notice any patterns? What happens to the rate of influenza in colder areas? What happens to islands?

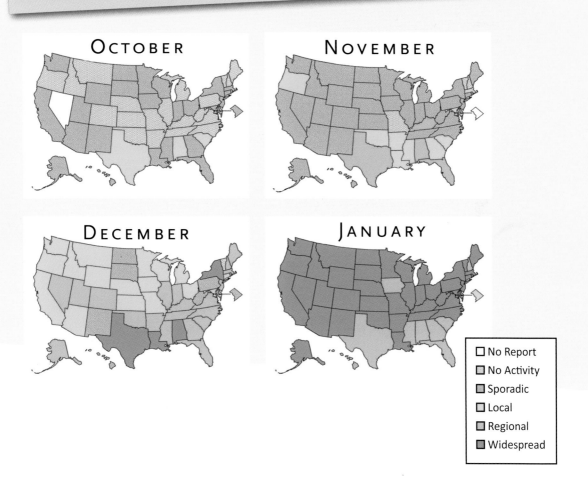

OCTOBER NOVEMBER

DECEMBER JANUARY

- ☐ No Report
- ☐ No Activity
- ☐ Sporadic
- ☐ Local
- ☐ Regional
- ☐ Widespread

CHAPTER 3

A HORRIFYING HISTORY

Humans have been subjected to deadly pandemics throughout history. The chances of pandemics happening increased as people formed larger communities, traded with their neighbors, explored new places, and went to war with each other. All of these activities made the spreading of viruses to larger groups of people more likely. Among the first pandemics was the bubonic plague.

By studying genetics, modern scientists discovered

that the bubonic plague bacteria appeared in China more than 2,600 years ago. Its natural reservoir was a rodent. Fleas spread the disease by biting a rodent and then biting a human.

Sometime in the 1320s or 1330s, the bubonic plague broke out again in China's Gobi Desert. This time it spread worldwide. Seagoing Chinese explorers introduced the disease to Europe and later to Africa. The bubonic plague became known as the Black Death because of black, bloody boils as big as apples that grew on the victim's skin. The plague could quickly spread from one person to another through the

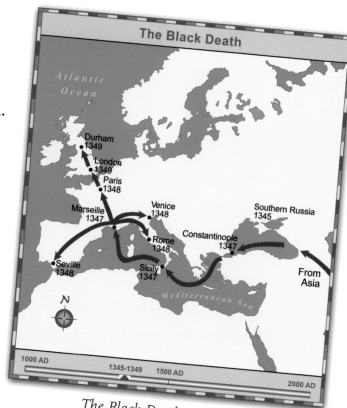

The Black Death swept through Europe in just a few years.

air. Without treatment, approximately half of the people who caught the plague died.

The Black Death swept across Europe in the 1340s. Trading, wars, and filthy conditions in towns and cities helped it spread. Ignorance about the disease also fueled its spread. There were people who believed that the plague was God's wrath. They thought they could escape the punishment by leaving their homes. They left behind sick family members and spread the disease to other areas. Within five years, the Black Death had killed about one-third of the European population— approximately 25 million people. It also killed many people in India and China.

Like the Black Death, smallpox ranks among the most devastating pandemics in human history. It emerged from India thousands of years ago and began spreading to every populated continent. Smallpox kills about a third of the people it infects. The virus can spread through contact or in the air.

SPREADING DISEASE ON PURPOSE

Bioterrorism involves the intentional release of disease-causing materials. It has been used for centuries. Mongol warriors flung plague-infected corpses at their enemies. Europeans purposely gave blankets infected with smallpox to Native Americans. In the 1930s, the Japanese army bombed China with plague fleas and infected clothing and supplies, killing around 400,000 people. Scientists prepare stockpiles of vaccines against diseases that could be used in bioterrorism today, such as anthrax.

Smallpox spread throughout Europe, Asia, and Africa by the 1500s. Sea travel and exploration then gave the disease a free ride to the western hemisphere. It killed millions of Native Americans. By the middle of the 1700s, smallpox was present everywhere in the world except for a few islands. During that century, smallpox killed as many as 400,000 people a year.

Finally a vaccine was developed, changing the course of history. In 1796, a scientist named Edward Jenner noticed women who milked cows seemed to be immune to smallpox. He wondered if this was because they were

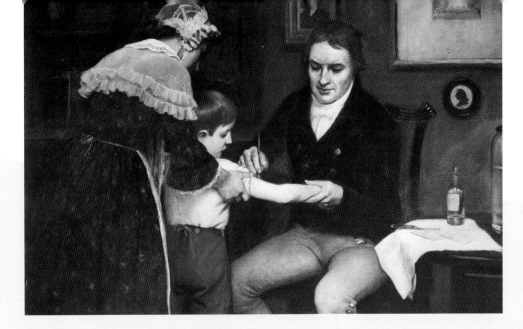

Jenner's work eventually led to the official 1979 declaration that smallpox had been eradicated from the planet.

exposed to cowpox, a disease related to smallpox but not as dangerous. To test his theory, Jenner injected cowpox into his gardener's young son and watched what happened. The boy got ill, but he quickly recovered. Then Jenner gave the boy a shot of smallpox virus. The boy did not get sick. Jenner had created a vaccine that would eventually wipe out one of the most devastating diseases in human history.

The worst pandemic in the last few decades has been acquired immunodeficiency syndrome (AIDS), caused by the human immunodeficiency virus (HIV). AIDS weakens a person's immune system, turning ordinary

THE SARS VIRUS

In 2002, there was a deadly pandemic known as severe acute respiratory syndrome (SARS). It infected more than 8,000 people and killed more than 700 people around the world. Scientists tried to locate the natural reservoir of the mysterious virus. Horseshoe bats in China were discovered to carry a virus related to the SARS virus. Chinese and Australian researchers used a special virus isolation technique. They studied the feces of the horseshoe bats. They found that the bat virus was 95 percent similar to the SARS virus that infects humans. In 2013, the team confirmed the bat was the origin of the virus responsible for the 2002 pandemic. Knowing the origin of the virus can help scientists create a vaccine and better prevention methods for SARS and other potential pandemics.

diseases into fatal illnesses. Since the AIDS pandemic broke out in the 1980s, it has killed approximately 36 million people. Another recent pandemic was the 2009 H1N1 influenza pandemic. About 61 million Americans became ill from H1N1, and about 12,470 died from it.

DETECTION AND TRACKING

The first people who broke out with the black boils of bubonic plague had no idea what had hit them until it was too late. But today, scientists have the knowledge and tools to detect, track, contain, manage, and even cure diseases. They are also learning how to prevent these diseases and wipe them out entirely.

For a virus to be identified and tracked, scientists must learn where it came from, where will it go next, and when it will get there. They also need to find out how a disease is transmitted from person to person, during which stages of a disease a person is able to infect others, and how the disease can be effectively treated.

When scientists discover a new virus, they use **genetic sequencers** to figure out what it is. Genetic sequencers show how similar a virus is to viruses that have been

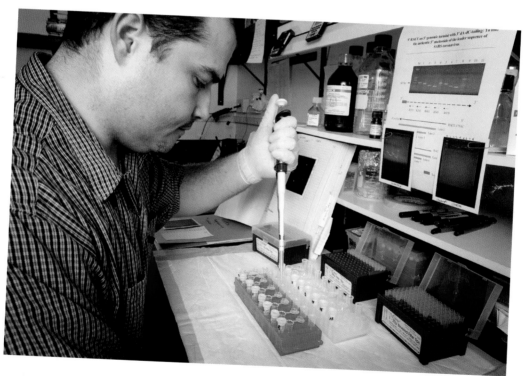

Determining how viruses are related can help scientists predict and prevent pandemics.

discovered before it. When a new virus appears, scientists can use this information to guess its effects and how it will spread. Viruses similar to already-known viruses may behave in similar ways. Thanks to genetic sequencing, it is becoming easier to identify and track new viruses.

Organizations such as the World Health Organization (WHO) watch and respond to health threats around the globe. One way they attempt to contain diseases is through isolation. People exposed to an infectious disease may be quarantined, or kept in a hospital apart from others. Even if they are not currently sick, they may become sick soon. Keeping them isolated stops a disease from spreading and becoming a pandemic.

Meanwhile, ordinary people can take steps to protect themselves and the people they know from pandemics. If a person gets sick, he or she can stay home from work or school. People can visit the doctor and receive treatment. People who live near mosquitoes and other insects can avoid bites by wearing proper clothing.

TRACKING VIRUSES

Nathan Wolfe is a virologist who is creating a pandemic early warning system. He founded Global Viral, an organization that promotes virus exploration and research. It also shares information. All around the world, scientists and staff members of Global Viral work together. They try to spot viruses as soon as they appear.

Scientists collect and record blood samples from people with diseases, study diseased wild animals, and document the course of diseases. They pay careful attention to groups of people who are more likely than others to become infected with a new virus. Wolfe believes that there is "nothing like on-the-ground information." His goal is to uncover and catch viruses before they can threaten us with another pandemic.

Travelers can learn about the risk of disease in the destinations they visit. And everyone can be vaccinated whenever possible. Finally, people can simply wash their hands frequently and practice good hygiene to prevent the spread of diseases.

BEATING DISEASES

The idea of a future pandemic similar to the Black Death or the 1918 flu is scary. With the dramatic increase in population in the 1900s and 2000s, the potential death toll from a pandemic has increased. However, the scientific community has grown too. Thanks to international research and sharing of information, it has become easier to prevent diseases from becoming widespread pandemics.

Many antibiotics were developed in the mid-1900s.

In the last century, science has won the battle against dozens of deadly diseases. Scientists have learned new ways to approach the treatment and prevention of diseases that could become pandemics. Polio, typhus, measles, rinderpest, and malaria are just some of the infectious diseases scientists have learned to prevent by vaccination. Other diseases can be defeated by **antibiotics**.

SUPERBUGS

Doctors have used antibiotics to cure bacterial infections since the 1800s. But antibiotics do not always work. Some bacteria adapt to resist even the strongest antibiotics. The resulting bacteria are often called superbugs. Some of these superbugs can spread quickly. To combat the spread of superbugs, doctors take extra care to keep hospitals clean. At the same time, scientists work to develop new kinds of antibiotics that will remain effective.

WHO and other organizations are working to develop a global tracking system for disease research and control. They use computer databases to tell scientists around the world about local outbreaks. The Internet and social media are also being used to help track the spread of diseases.

Another goal of WHO is to help developing nations prevent pandemics. Disease outbreaks are more common and harder to contain in developing nations. Global efforts are needed to help poorer nations prevent the spread of diseases. WHO works to provide these nations with safe water supplies, better ways to deal with waste, and vaccination programs.

In some countries, flu shots are becoming more than just an option. They are required in some places, such

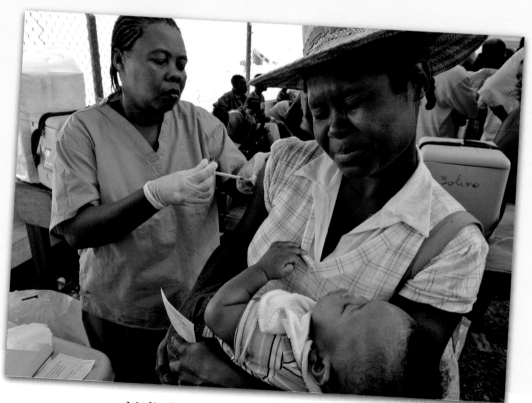

Medical workers helped vaccinate people in Haiti after the devastating earthquake in 2010.

as schools and hospitals. This is because when enough people are immunized against a virus, together they form what is known as herd immunity. Once a certain percentage of people in a community are immunized, diseases have a much smaller chance of spreading and becoming a pandemic.

Human beings have faced powerful microscopic enemies throughout history. These tiny killers have managed to survive, change, become resistant to drugs, and kill millions of people. But every day, science gets a step closer to winning the war against pandemics.

HERD IMMUNITY

The diagram at right shows how herd immunity works. Using the diagram and the text from this chapter, explain herd immunity in your own words. Why is this idea so important in preventing pandemics?

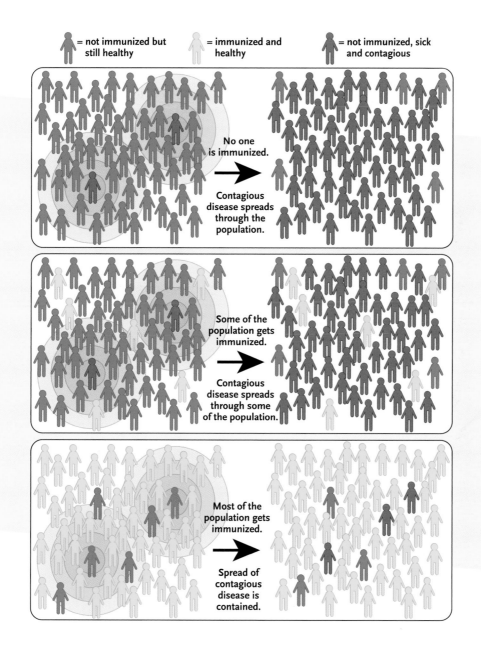

= not immunized but still healthy

= immunized and healthy

= not immunized, sick and contagious

No one is immunized. → Contagious disease spreads through the population.

Some of the population gets immunized. → Contagious disease spreads through some of the population.

Most of the population gets immunized. → Spread of contagious disease is contained.

TOP FIVE WORST PANDEMICS

1. **Smallpox**
   Smallpox is a contagious virus that killed between 90 and 95 million Native American people. These deaths took place between the 1400s and 1800s. Native Americans caught the disease from European settlers who came to the Americas.

2. **Cholera**
   This bacterial disease existed in India since ancient times. The rest of the world was exposed when trade grew between India and other countries in the early 1800s. More than 100,000 people still die each year from cholera.

3. **Tuberculosis**
   Tuberculosis is a bacterial disease that destroys the lungs. It has affected humans throughout recorded history. It has been discovered in Egyptian mummies, and ancient Greek authors wrote about its effects.

4. **The Black Death**
   Also known as the bubonic plague, the Black Death is believed to be one of the first pandemics. It killed approximately one-third of Europe's population.

5. **Malaria**
   There are records of malaria dating back more than 4,000 years. The disease is spread by mosquitoes. Today there are hundreds of millions of cases of malaria in sub-Saharan Africa.

FURTHER READING

Gardy, Jennifer. *It's Catching: The Infectious World of Germs and Microbes.* Berkeley, CA: Owlkids Books, 2014.

Marciniak, Kristin. *The Flu Pandemic of 1918.* Minneapolis, MN: Abdo, 2014.

Piddock, Charles. *Outbreak: Science Seeks Safeguards for Global Health.* Washington, DC: National Geographic, 2008.

WEB SITES

National Institute of Environmental Health Sciences—Pandemic Flu
http://kids.niehs.nih.gov/explore/hliving/pandemic_flu.htm
This Web site includes information about how to prevent the flu. It also tells how you can stay safe if a pandemic occurs.

Rice University—Medical Mysteries
http://medmyst.rice.edu
This interactive Web site features games that provide a fun and interesting way to learn about infectious diseases.

GLOSSARY

antibiotics (an-ti-bye-OT-ikss) drugs used to kill bacteria

contagious (kuhn-TAY-juhss) spread by direct contact with someone or something infected with a disease

contaminated (kuhn-TAM-uh-nay-tid) dirty or unfit for use

genetic sequencers (juh-NET-ik SEE-kwuhnss-er) equipment used to study the genetic code of a virus or organism

immune system (i-MYOON SISS-tuhm) the natural body function that protects people against disease

infectious (in-FEK-shuhss) able to spread from one person to another

influenza (in-floo-EN-zuh) also known as flu; an infectious disease caused by a virus that causes fever, pain, weakness, and breathing problems

microbe (MYE-krobe) a living thing too small to see without a microscope

vectors (VEK-tuhrz) living things that transmit diseases from one animal or plant to another

INDEX